# CHILDREN'S ENCYCLOPEDIA
## THE WORLD OF KNOWLEDGE

# LIFE SCIENCES

Manasvi Vohra

V&S PUBLISHERS

*Published by:*

F-2/16, Ansari road, Daryaganj, New Delhi-110002
☎ 23240026, 23240027 • *Fax:* 011-23240028
*Email:* info@vspublishers.com • *Website:* www.vspublishers.com

**Regional Office : Hyderabad**
5-1-707/1, Brij Bhawan (Beside Central Bank of India Lane)
Bank Street, Koti, Hyderabad - 500 095
☎ 040-24737290
*E-mail:* vspublishershyd@gmail.com

**Branch Office : Mumbai**
Jaywant Industrial Estate, 1st Floor–108, Tardeo Road
Opposite Sobo Central Mall, Mumbai – 400 034
☎ 022-23510736
*E-mail:* vspublishersmum@gmail.com

Follow us on:

© Copyright: *V&S PUBLISHERS*
**Edition 2018**

---

### DISCLAIMER

While every attempt has been made to provide accurate and timely information in this book, neither the author nor the publisher assumes any responsibility for errors, unintended omissions or commissions detected therein. The author and publisher makes no representation or warranty with respect to the comprehensiveness or completeness of the contents provided.

All matters included have been simplified under professional guidance for general information only, without any warranty for applicability on an individual. Any mention of an organization or a website in the book, by way of citation or as a source of additional information, doesn't imply the endorsement of the content either by the author or the publisher. It is possible that websites cited may have changed or removed between the time of editing and publishing the book.

Results from using the expert opinion in this book will be totally dependent on individual circumstances and factors beyond the control of the author and the publisher.

It makes sense to elicit advice from well informed sources before implementing the ideas given in the book. The reader assumes full responsibility for the consequences arising out from reading this book.

For proper guidance, it is advisable to read the book under the watchful eyes of parents/guardian. The buyer of this book assumes all responsibility for the use of given materials and information.

The copyright of the entire content of this book rests with the author/publisher. Any infringement/transmission of the cover design, text or illustrations, in any form, by any means, by any entity will invite legal action and be responsible for consequences thereon.

---

Printed at Repro Knowledgecast Limited, Thane

# PUBLISHER'S NOTE

**V&S Publishers** is glad to announce the launch of a unique, set of 12 books under the head, *Children's Encyclopedia – The World of Knowledge.* The set of 12 books namely – *Physices, Chemistry, Space Science, General Sceince, Life Science, Human Body, Electronics & Communications, Scientists, Inventions & Discoveries, Transportation, The Earth, and GK (General Knowledge)* has been especially developed keeping in mind the students and children of all age groups, particularly from 6 to 14 years of age. Our main aim is to arouse the interest and solve the queries of the school children regarding the various and diverse topics of Science and help them master the subject thoroughly.

In the book, *Life Sciences* the author has broadlydealt wit some interesting and fascinating Scientific facts like *What is Life Science, Animal Kingdom, Plant Kingdom Kingdom, Classification of Plants and Animals,* etc.

Each chapter is followed by a section called **Quick Facts** that contains a set of interesting and fascinating facts about the topics already discussed in the chapter. There are also **Exercises** compiled at the end of the book followed by a **Glossary** of difficult words and scientific terms to make the book complete and comprehensive.

## Quick Facts

- A poison arrow frog has so much poison in it that it can harm about 2200 people in one squirt.

Though our aim is to be flawless, but errors might have crept in inadvertently. So we request our esteemed readers to read the book thoroughly and offer valuable suggestions wherever necessary to improve and enhance the quality of the book. Hope it interests you all and serves its purpose well.

# CONTENTS

Introduction : What is Life Science?  7

**Part - I : Animal Kingdom**     11

Chapter 1 : Anatomy   13

Chapter 2 : Animal Classification   21

Chapter 3 : Animal Behaviour   31

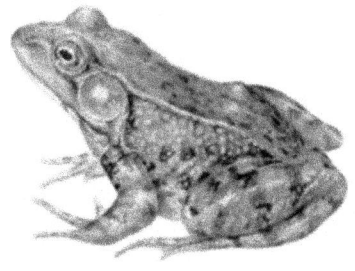

**Part - II : Plant Kingdom**       43

Chapter 1 : Parts of a Plant        45

Chapter 2 : Photosynthesis        49

Chapter 3 : Growth and Development  52

Chapter 4 : Plant Classification      59

**Exercises**   67

**Glossary**   71

# Introduction

## WHAT IS LIFE SCIENCE?

Millions of things surround us. We distinguish these things and the world around us as living and non-living based on the similarities that each of these possess. The scientific study of living beings is called *life science*.

Living beings possess special characteristics that make them different from non-living things. They are as follows:

### (i) They Move

Unlike non-living things, living things can *move from one place to another* in search of food, shelter, protection against enemies, and favourable weather conditions.

Animals use their legs to move, birds and insects use their wings, fishes swim, and snakes crawl.

*A Polar Bear on the Move*

*An Insect on a Flower*

*Bird Flying*

Although plants do not move, they are considered as living things as their parts show movements. The best example of this is how a sunflower turns towards the sun, a touch-me-not closes its leaves when touched, and a poppy flower closes its petals at night and opens them in the morning.

*A Snake Crawling*

## (ii) They Grow

*Seeds Germinating*

Living things grow and change their shape as they develop. Plants develop from seeds; animals grow from eggs or from a foetus.

*Hatching of An Egg*

## (iii) They Breathe

Living things breathe to remain alive. Human beings have a nose to breathe. Some insects have air holes to breathe. Fishes have gills, whereas plants have stomata to breathe.

*Snakes Respire through Skin*

*A Human Nose*

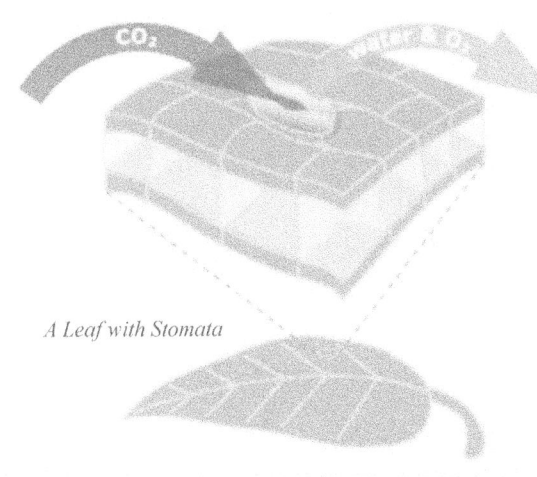
*A Leaf with Stomata*

### (iv) They Need Food

Living things require food to grow. Plants produce their own food through the process of *photosynthesis* and animals feed on plants or other animals to survive.

*Cows Grazing in the Open Field*

### (v) They Feel

Living beings have sense organs. They can feel pain, smell their food and feel the changes happening around them. Though plants do not have any sense organs, they respond to the changes in their environment, which proves that they too feel.

*Sunflowers Facing the Sun*

### (vi) They Reproduce

Reproduction forms a major process in the lives of living things. They multiply. Plants produce seeds that grow into new plants. Animals give birth to young ones that help in continuing their life cycle.

*A Young Animal with its Mother*

### (vii) They Perish

Every living being ceases to exist after some time. Age, harsh weather, climate change, diseases and natural calamities, such as droughts, floods, etc., are the main reasons for the destruction or death of the living things.

*A Withered Plant*

# Part - I

# ANIMAL KINGDOM

Apart from the human race, there are other living things on the planet, earth that make it a more beautiful place to live in. One among them is the Animal Kingdom. There are thousands of species, most of them similar to each other, while there are others, who are completely different. They are mostly classified based on their similarities, for example – **Vertebrates** (those with a backbone) and **Invertebrates** (those without a spinal column or a backbone). Below, you will learn a lot more about different characteristics of animals, their classifications, their body systems and much more.

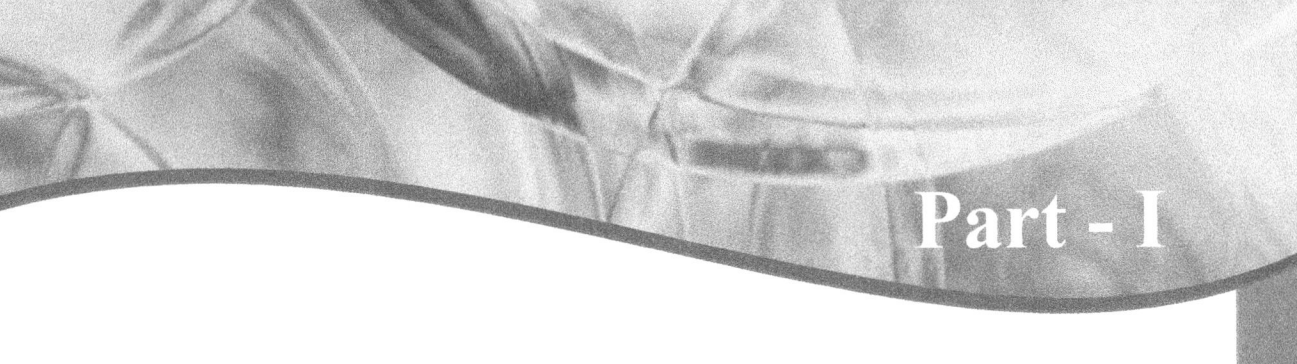

# Chapter - 1

# ANATOMY

## Body Systems

Several *body systems* make the body of an animal work. In most animals, (vertebrates and invertebrates), there are two major body systems:

(i) The *muscular system*

(ii) The *skeletal system*

The muscular system helps in the movement of the body using muscles and the skeletal system provides structural support to the system and protects the body. These together form the **body weight**.

Apart from these, there are various other systems. These are as follows:

## Digestive System

The digestive system breaks the food down to produce energy. Majority of the animals use their mouth to take in food. This process is called **ingestion**.

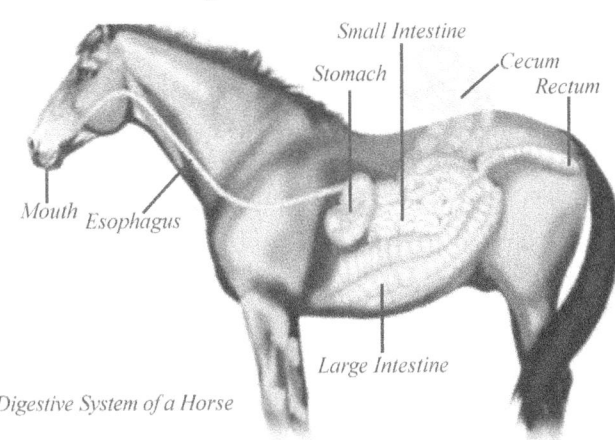

*Digestive System of a Horse*

Some animals like tapeworms, live in the digestive system of another animal and take in nutrients from that animal directly through their body walls.

Oysters and mussels feed on small organisms and particles from the surrounding water.

Earthworms and termites eat the dirt or wood they burrow through.

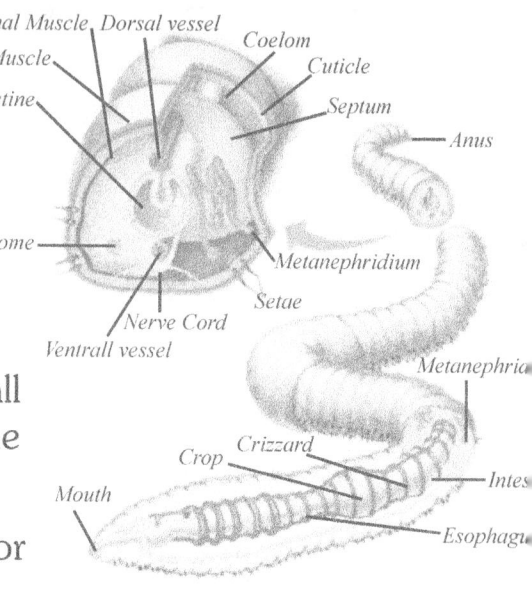

*Digestive System of an Earthworm*

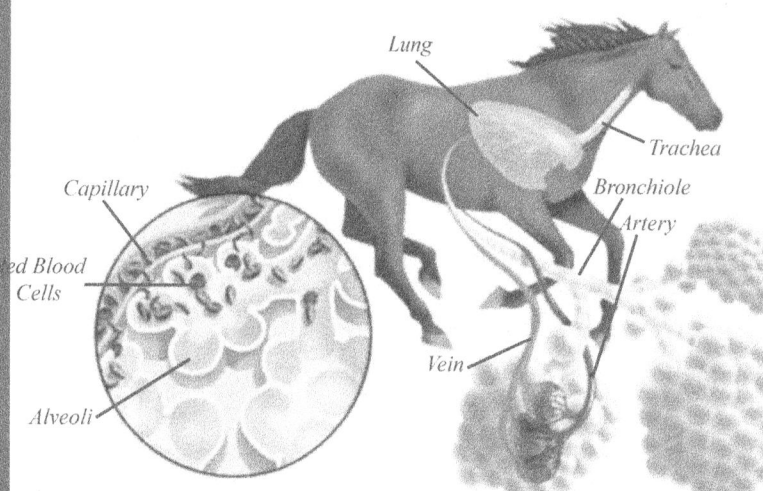

*Respiratory System in a Horse*

# Respiratory System

The respiratory system removes carbon dioxide, which is harmful to the body, produced during the production of energy.

Simple invertebrates lack respiratory organs, whereas in amphibians, lungs and skin both serve as respiratory organs.

An elephant can breathe through its mouth as well as its trunk, so it can survive under water holding its trunk above the water level.

*An Elephant Breathing through its Trunk*

## Circulatory System

The circulatory system circulates blood in the body, along with oxygen and carbon dioxide.

*Circulatory System of a Fish*

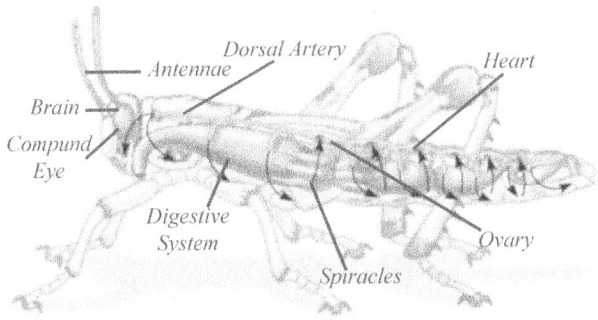
*Circulatory System in a Grasshopper*

Most vertebrates have a closed cardiovascular system, which means that the blood circulates through arteries, veins and capillaries.

Some invertebrates have an open cardiovascular system.

## Excretory System

The excretory system removes the waste from the body.

Marine bony fishes suffer from a higher rate of water loss. To compensate this loss, they

*Excretory System of Bony Fish*

drink a lot of seawater. The excess salt taken in by drinking the salty seawater is removed through specialised cells in its gills.

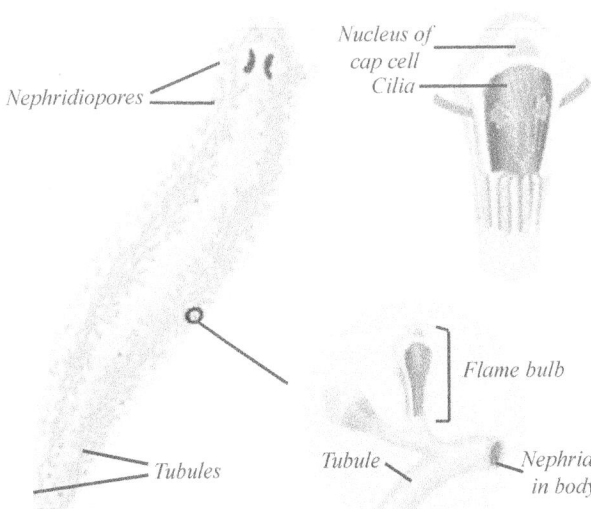
*Excretory System of an Earthworm*

## Nervous System

The nervous system processes information and makes the body react.

The sensory organs of the animals help them to react and respond to their environment. It helps them to coordinate the various systems in their bodies to attack their prey or escape from their attackers. The nervous system prompts them to escape or provide their muscles, the increased blood supply to run and attack. The respiratory system then provides the oxygen needed on account of the increased activity and once the prey is caught, the digestive system helps to digest the food.

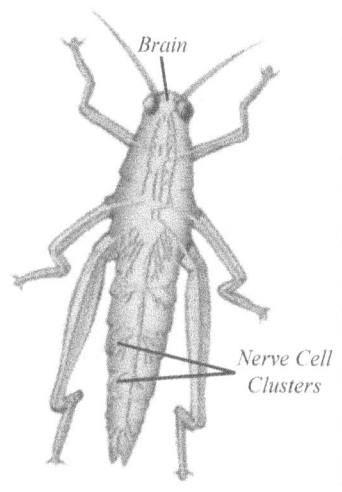

*Nervous System of a Cockroach*

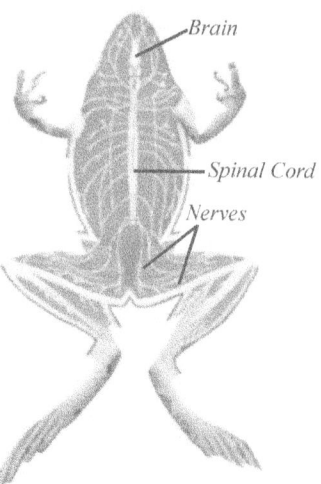

*Nervous System of a Frog*

## Endocrine System

The endocrine system works with the nervous system to produce hormones or chemical substances helpful for coordination of body processes.

Mostly, animals with well-developed nervous and circulatory systems have an endocrine system. Animals have to constantly adapt to changes in the environment. The nervous and endocrine systems together help the animal to adapt to their ever-changing and new environment.

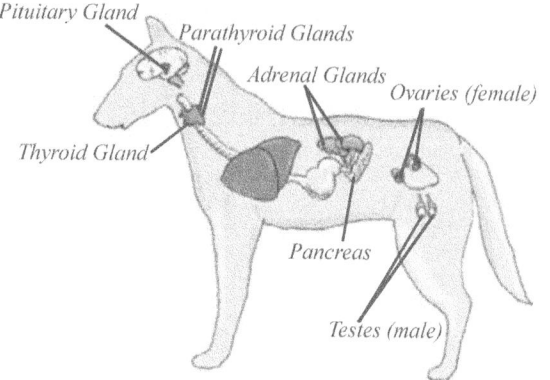

*Endocrine System of a Dog*

*An English Bulldog*

## Reproductive System

The reproductive system helps to produce the young ones.

Birds, chickens and turtles lay eggs in which the young ones continue to develop. Once developed, these eggs hatch to give rise to the young ones.

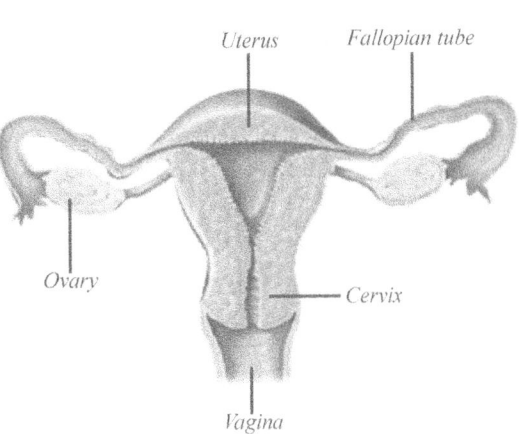

*Reproductive System in Mammals*

*A Hen Laying Eggs*

Most mammals develop within the mother and are later given birth. Garter snakes and Madagascar hissing cockroaches lay eggs that hatch as soon as they are laid.

### Quick Facts

- **The memory span of a goldfish is 3 seconds.**
- **A cow's sweat glands are in its nose.**
- **Lobsters have pale-blue coloured blood.**

## Skeleton and Muscles

The skeleton protects the organs of the body and in some animals, it serves as an external covering.

The external skeleton or **exoskeleton** is usually found in invertebrates, providing

*Exoskeleton of an Arachnid (Arthropod)*

them a protective covering, guarding their organs and soft tissues. Since it is difficult to grow the exoskeleton, the animals have to shed it every now and then. This external skeleton makes the body very heavy and is therefore, usually found in animals smaller in size and also in bigger animals living underwater, as the weight becomes less and manageable under water.

**Endoskeleton** or internal skeleton, found in most vertebrates, not only protects and gives form to the body, but also connects with the muscles, providing them the energy needed. Animals without limbs, such as earthworms and jellyfish, contract and expand their muscles to move forward, whereas those with limbs move using their muscles to push their limbs front, back, up or down.

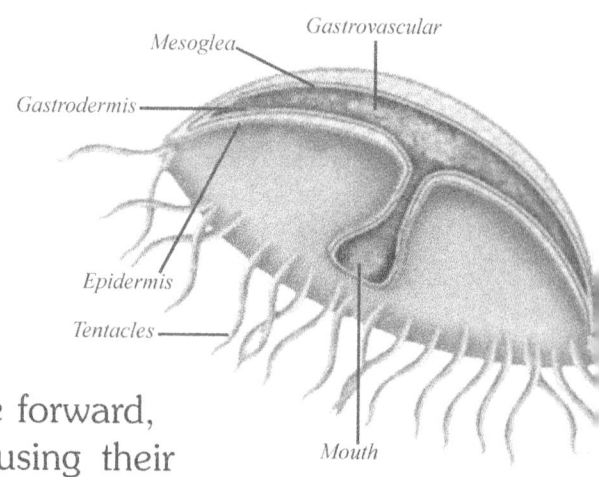

Endoskeleton of a Jellyfish

## Quick Facts

- Cats cannot move their jaws sideways.
- A cat has 32 muscles in each ear.
- A bear has 42 teeth; a mosquito has 47 teeth.
- A jelly fish is 95% water.

## Body Coverings

The animal body is covered with some kind of covering. In mammals, this covering is formed by the dead skin, whereas in insects, it is formed by hard proteins and water-resistant wax.

Animal with Scales (Chameleon)

18

Mammals have their bodies covered with extra-protective

*Animal with Fur (Otter)*

*Animals with Feathers (Cock)*

coverings in the form of scales, feathers, fur, hair and bristles. Fur and feathers help to prevent the body heat from escaping. Coloured body coverings and patterns help to provide camouflage and attract mates.

*Animals with Hair*

## Quick Facts

- The spines of a porcupine are so light that when put in water, it floats.
- One can differentiate a male giraffe from a female by looking at its horns; a cow giraffe (female) has shorter horns with hair on its tips, whereas a bull giraffe (male) has longer and plain horns without hair.
- The red colour in the skin of a hippopotamus is a substance that protects it from sunburns.

## Senses

Senses are as useful to animals as they are to human beings. Animals need their senses to find their food and their ways. However, some animals have developed unique methods to find their ways around.

Whales, bats and dolphins are very sensitive to echolocation – they have a very strong sense of hearing that helps them navigate around and hunt for food. Though their vision is weak, they can judge their ways by sounds being reflected from the surroundings.

*A Bat*

Snails have eyes on two long stalks and can turn them all around to see, and flip them inside out to shut them.

Snakes can stick out their tongues and smell the air.

Cows have four times more taste buds than human beings.

*Snail*

*Frog*   *Birds*

Frogs can see what is behind them without turning their heads.

Birds can't move their eyes but can turn their whole heads to look around. They have twice as many bones in their necks as human beings do.

## Quick Facts

- A goat has rectangular pupils.
- A scallop has 35 blue eyes.
- A chameleon's tongue is twice the length of its body.

# Chapter - 2

# ANIMAL CLASSIFICATION

There are millions of animals around us. With almost two million species of animals identified till date, their study becomes easier by classifying or grouping them into various categories. The classification of animals is known as **taxonomy**.

Scientists classify organisms according to their *kingdoms, phylum or phyla, classes, orders, families, genus* and *species*. While most of the animals can move; some like sea squirts spend their adult life in one place, but as young ones, they can move around freely. They can also be distinguished by their basic biological features.

Animals are broadly classified into the following two groups:

(i) Vertebrates

(ii) Invertebrates

Animals that have a backbone are called vertebrates and invertebrates include animals which do not have a backbone. Even though vertebrates are more commonly known, they are fewer in number as compared to the invertebrates. Unlike vertebrates, the invertebrates have very less features in common with each other except their lack of backbone.

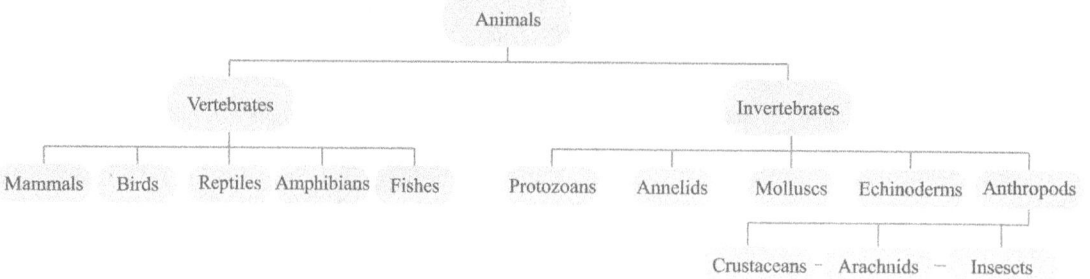

## (i) Vertebrates

Vertebrates are divided into the following five main groups:

(a) Mammals

(b) Birds

(c) Reptiles

(d) Amphibians

(e) Fishes

### (a) Mammals

Mammals are so called because they feed and nourish their young ones on the milk produced by the mother's mammary glands. They are mostly found on land.

Giraffe

Cow

Monkeys

*Kangaroo*

They adapt very easily to their surroundings, making them the most commonly found animal group. They have the ability to maintain their body temperatures against the changing outside weather. Some animals, such as the *duck-billed platypus* and the *echidna* lay eggs even though they are mammals. On the other hand, there are mammals like *kangaroos* that give birth to the young ones like any other mammal, but they give birth at a very early stage, making their offspring undernourished. They have to carry their young ones in their pouches and nourish them with their milk.

*Duck-Billed Platypus*

## (b) Birds

The characteristic feature of birds is their ability to fly. Their wings, feathers, and light, streamlined bodies help them fly to far-off places. However, there are birds, such as the *ostriches* that cannot fly. These warm-blooded animals reproduce by laying eggs. They are known to be brilliant architects. A *weaver bird* uses grass, twigs and leaves to weave its nest using its beak. It creates an opening at the bottom of the nest to enter into its home. *Tailor birds* too make their nests

*A Weaver Bird Weaving its Nest*

*A Bird Flying*

*An Ostrich is a Flightless Bird*

23

by sewing large leaves using cotton thread and its beak as a needle. At the same time, there are birds like the cuckoo that does not build its own nest and lays its eggs in the nests of other birds.

*A Tailor Bird and its Nest*

## (c) Reptiles

Snakes, lizards, crocodiles, alligators, tortoises and turtles form the group of animals called the *reptiles*. These are *egg-laying animals*. They live mainly in water and lay their eggs on land. They are *cold-blooded vertebrates* that have a tough skin covered with scales.

*Crocodile*

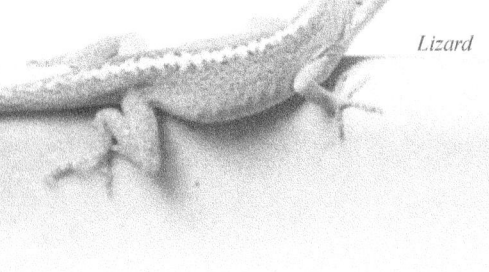
*Lizard*

*Tortoise*

## (d) Amphibians

Amphibians are classified as animals that live both on land as well as in water. Newts, salamanders, frogs and toads are some of these cold-blooded vertebrates. They start as larvae under water, breathing through gills, and as adults, live on land and take in oxygen through lungs. (Their body temperatures change according to the outside temperatures.

*Frog*

*Salamander*

## (e) Fishes

Fishes are known to be the *first backboned animals* to appear on the earth. A typical fish breathes or respires through gills, has a body covered with scales, moves using fins, and is a cold-blooded vertebrate. They are either freshwater bound or inhabitants of the sea. However, there are a few species that switch between the two environments.

*Gills of a Fish*

*Shark*

### Quick Facts

- A housefly can live for only 14 days.
- The octopus has three hearts.
- A starfish is the only animal that can turn its stomach inside out.

## (ii) Invertebrates

The invertebrates are divided into five major groups:

(a) Protozoans  
(b) Annelids  
(c) Molluscs  
(d) Echinoderms  
(e) Arthropods

Arthropods can be further divided into the following three groups:
- Crustaceans
- Arachnids
- Insects

## (a) Protozoans

Protozoans are single-celled animals that are so small that they can only be seen under a microscope. They have the ability to move and reproduce like any multi-cellular animal.

*Amoeba* and *flagellates* are types of protozoa. They form a vital link of the food chain. They feed on algae and bacteria by either absorbing them through their cell membranes or by consuming them through their mouth-like openings. Then they themselves become the food for the fishes and other animals. They have stomach-like structures called *vacuoles* to digest their food.

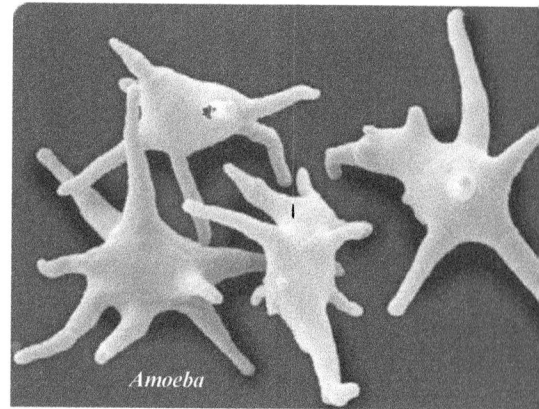

*Amoeba*

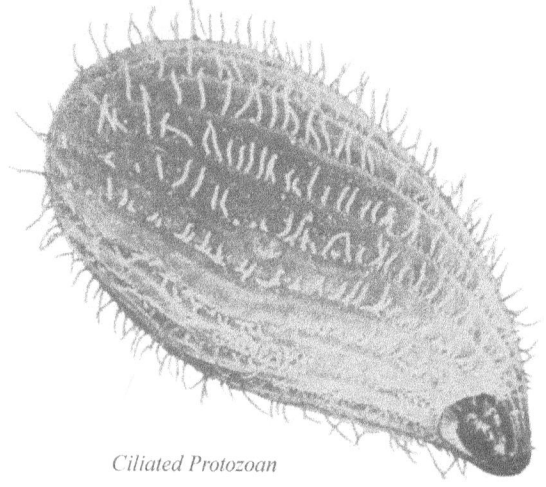

*Ciliated Protozoan*

They even respire or breathe through their cell membranes and reproduce by splitting their bodies into half.

## (b) Annelids

Thousands of species of annelids have been discovered till date. These include some known *worms* and *leeches*. Their sizes range from a few inches to a hundred feet. Their bodies are divided into *segments* and have well-developed internal organs. They have *no limbs*.

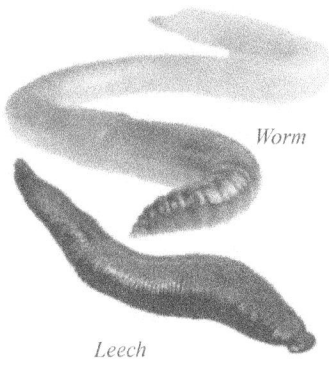
*Worm*
*Leech*

## (c) Molluscs

Fossils over millions of years old have proven that molluscs were one of the *first organisms on the Earth*. They have soft bodies covered with hard shells. Some molluscs, such as *snails* and *slugs* can be found on land, whereas molluscs, such as *oysters*, *mussels*, *clams*, *squids* and *octopuses* are found under water. Molluscs living on land have flat soles, which help them move, whereas those living in water move forward by pumping out water using their bodies.

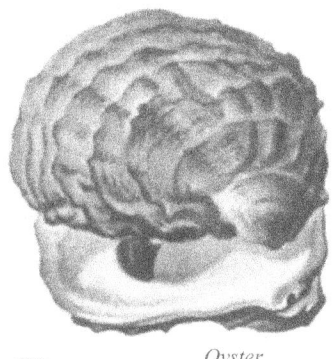
*Octopus*
*Oyster*
*Squid*

## (d) Echinoderms

Marine animals that live in the ocean are called echinoderms. *Starfish*, *sea urchin*, *sand dollar*, and *sea cucumber* are some well-known echinoderms. The central part of the body contains the spine, mouth and other organs.

*Sea Cucumber*

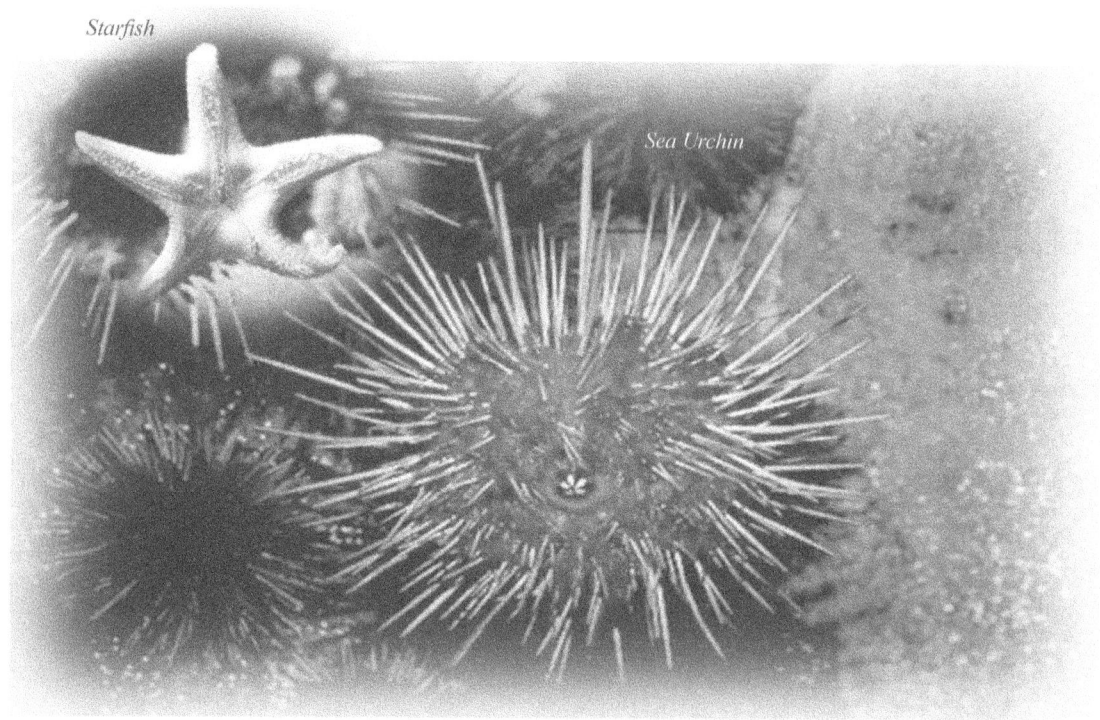

### (e) Arthropods

- *Crustaceans*

Crustaceans are mostly found in the oceans or other water bodies. The most commonly known crustaceans are the *crabs*, *lobsters* and *barnacles*. Their bodies are covered by hard, external shells, which protect their bodies. Their heads have antennae which form a part of their sensory system. Their legs help them crawl and swim. Many crustaceans have claws that help them crawl or eat.

- *Arachnids*

*Spiders*, *scorpions*, *ticks* and *mites* are some commonly known arachnids. They too have a hard

*Spider*

external skeleton. Most arachnids like the spiders have eight legs that help them to walk. Most spiders have eight eyes and fangs that can inject poison into their prey. Scorpions are also arachnids, and also have eight legs, and a pair of pincers for catching and holding their prey. However, they use their tails to sting their enemies. *Mites* and *ticks* are small, parasitic arachnids that live on the blood and tissue fluid of other animals and can occasionally transmit diseases.

### Insects

Insects form the largest group of arthropods. They include the fly, mosquito, beetle, butterfly, moth, dragonfly and bee. Insects have a hard external

*Dragonfly*

*Fly*

*Moth*

skeleton that covers their bodies. This makes it difficult for their cover to grow as they grow. Hence, they have to shed their exoskeleton regularly. The insect's head has a pair of antennae and compound eyes, which means they have many lenses for each eye, gifting them with good eyesight. They may also have wings.

## Quick Facts

- The largest frog in the world is the Goliath frog.
- A woodpecker can peck 20 times per second.
- The smallest mammal in the world is the bumblebee bat found in Thailand. It weighs less than a penny.
- Vertebrates are further divided into the following five main groups:
  * Mammals: Monkeys, Human Beings, Bats, Cows, Dogs, etc.
  * Birds—Tailor Bird, Weaver Bird, Ostrich, etc.
  * Reptiles –Snakes, Lizards, Tortoises and many more.
  * Amphibians—Frogs, Salamanders, etc.
  * There ar more species of fish than all the species of amphibians, reptiles, birds and mammals.
  * The largest fish is the great whale shark which can reach upto 50 feet in length, and the smallest fish is the Philippine goby that is less than 1/3 of an inch when fully grown.
  * Prawns and sharks are also grouped under fishes.

# Chapter - 3

# ANIMAL BEHAVIOUR

## Habitat

A habitat is the place where an animal lives. A habitat, in ecological terms is called a **biome**. It provides the animal with food, water and shelter, i.e., almost everything, it needs to survive. Based on where they live, animals can be classified as:

- *Terrestrial*
- *Aquatic*
- *Arboreal*
- *Amphibians*
- *Aerial*

*Terrestrial* animals live primarily on the ground, unlike *arboreal* animals that live on trees or *aerial* animals that are airborne. Aquatic animals live in water, whereas amphibians live both on land as well as in water. However, a clear divide like this can be often misleading. There are many animals, such as penguins and seals, which live on land and derive their food from water, and yet are classified as terrestrial animals. Also, there are many animals that spend half of their life cycle in water, such as frogs. They give birth and grow in water and spend their adult life on land.

## Adapting to the Habitat

Some animals are capable of adapting to different environments and climates, yet they are mostly bound to one habitat. Grasslands serve as a major habitat for many animals. These regions receive

*Desert Animals in their Natural Habitat*

more rainfall than the deserts, making them not too dry, and less rainfall than the rainforests, making them not wet enough for dense vegetation. Grasslands are mainly covered by tall or short grass and non-woody plants, but also sometimes by woody plants, trees and shrubs. They are favourable for animals, whose lives depend upon grazing and can digest the grass well. Their roots serve as a potential source of food for the many animals and insects living in this habitat. The root system also holds the soil together, reducing

*Grassland Animals in their Natural Habitat*

the chances of it caving in, and thus, providing burrowing animals with a home. However, grasslands make it difficult for animals to hide, exposing them to predators and increasing the risk of being attacked. Also, it is dangerous for the young ones, who are at greater risks of being attacked or trampled under the feet of the animals grazing in the grasses. Other such habitats are formed by deserts, forests, mountains, Polar regions, rivers and wetlands, coral reefs and urban areas.

## Homes

Animals build or use the existing, natural or man-made homes to live. However, their purpose of choosing a home may differ. Rock caves, for instance, are used by several animals for varied reasons depending on their habitats or habits. They protect the tigers from heat, provide shelter to brown bears living in the

Hives

Burrows

*Nests*

*Caves*

*Tree homes*

mountainous regions, help certain animals (Moray eels) to hide and attack their prey, and protect a bat from the daylight. Other types of homes for animals are burrows, tree homes, hives, nests, etc.

## Effects of Change

Animals learn to adapt to the changing times and climate. However, an animal cannot adapt very quickly in an alien habitat and would hence, cease to survive. The environmental and climatic changes, taken place over the years, affecting the habitats, have thus led to the extinction of many species of animals and are still pushing many to the verge of extinction.

## Migration

Migration is the seasonal or annual journey of animals in search of better living conditions. It could be because of the availability of food, seasonal change, mating opportunities, etc. Some animals, such as the White-throated Dipper, which changes the altitudinal levels to escape the cold, migrate to shorter distances, whereas many animals, such as the Arctic terns, which travel between Poles, cover greater distances. After staying in the new habitat for a short while, the migratory animals return to their original habitat. The Canada geese, for instance, travel to the Arctic Circle in the spring and return to warmer places in the south during autumn. However, a Monarch butterfly never completes its migratory cycle on its own. It reproduces on its journey and then the journey is carried on by its next generations.

*Monarch Butterfly*

*Artic Terns*

## Quick Facts

- Antarctica is the only continent that does not have reptiles or snakes.
- Penguins live to the south of the equator.
- Apart from the few protected in the national parks of Gir, India, and other such artificial or man-made environments, lions are now naturally found only in Africa.

## HUNTING AND FEEDING

### Food habits

*Carnivores*

Animals obtain energy from food. Those animals that survive by feeding on other animals, either as *predators* or as *scavengers*, are called **carnivores**.

*Herbivores*

**Predators** hunt and kill other animals for food, while **scavengers** feed on the carcass or body of already dead animals. The characteristic features of predators, such as sharp teeth and claws, make it possible for them to hunt for

*Omnivores*   *Scavengers*

*Parasites*

food. Carnivorous animals, such as tigers, lions, crocodiles, snakes and frogs are predators, whereas vultures, spotted hyenas, flesh flies, and coyotes are scavengers. The animals that feed on plant matter are **herbivores**. Most domestic animals like cows, buffaloes, donkeys, etc. are herbivorous animals. However, there are some animals that feed on both plants and animals. Such animals are called **omnivores**. There are also animals that feed on other living organisms. They are called **parasites**.

## Defence Mechanisms

It is the basic nature of every living being to develop defence mechanisms to protect themselves from danger. Escaping the threat by using their speed, spitting venom, using their bright coloured bodies to distract their attackers, or going into hiding are some of the defence mechanisms used by animals. The other method is camouflage, where an animal changes its colour to blend itself with the colour of its environment. Chameleons and octopuses have the ability to change colour to merge with their surroundings, making them invisible to their predators. A herd of zebras moving together can form a brilliant camouflage, as their stripes together look like a giant mass of black and white stripes, making it difficult for the predator to spot an individual zebra. A puffer fish inflates its body, making pointed spines stick out, and thus, it becomes difficult to attack it.

*Chameleon*

*A Puffer Fish*

*Herd of Zebras*

## Quick Facts

- A poison arrow frog has so much poison in it that it can harm about 2200 people in one squirt.
- No two zebras have exactly the same stripes.
- Dolphins do not drink the water of the sea in which they live, but acquire water from feeding on water-rich food, such as sea cucumbers and squids.
- Tigers have retractable claws, which means they can take in and bring out their claws when needed.

## Birth and Development

Reproduction forms an important process in the life of any living being. It helps the species to multiply and evolve. Animals reproduce in the following two ways:

(i) Asexually

(ii) Sexually

In asexual reproduction, an animal does not require a partner. It divides its own body to give birth to a young one. The biggest disadvantage of this method is that the newly formed animal is exactly like its parent, making them vulnerable to all the dangers and diseases that the parent faces.

In sexual reproduction, an animal usually finds another animal of its kind, usually of the opposite gender, and they together produce a young one that has the qualities of both the parents. This induces variety in the species, but makes it difficult for the mother, as she is the only one who has to give birth to the baby. Some animals lay

*Animals with their Young Ones*

eggs that hatch into young ones, whereas some directly give birth to the younger animals. In such cases, the newborns are generally undernourished and are fed the milk of their mothers.

## Quick Facts

- If the eggs are incubated at over 33°c, then the egg hatches into a male or 'bull' crocodile. At lower temperatures, only female or 'cow' crocodiles develop.
- Pandas, when born are as tiny as rats but, grow fully when they reach the age of four.
- A male penguin warms the egg laid by the female penguin without eating or feeding, and in the process loses 40 percent of its weight.

*Whale*

*Glow Worm with its Tail Light on*

## Communication

Communication is important for survival. All animals communicate to their own kind in different ways. Apart from the most common ways of communication, such as facial expression and eye contact, animals use some specific ways, such as light, sound, and even scent as a means of communication. Glow worms, for instance, turn their light on to attract their potential mates. Many animals use sound to communicate, such as from small creatures like crickets to large ones, such as whales. Animals that get separated from their herd in the grassland find their way back by smelling the scent trails left by the hoofs of those in the herd. However, these methods of communication can often draw the enemies closer and thus, prove to be a disadvantage.

### Quick Facts

- Giraffes have no vocal chords and cats have 100 vocal chords.
- An injured or sick dolphin's cries can make other dolphins arrive to help raise it to the surface of the water so that it becomes easy for the dolphin to breathe.
- Blue and fin whales can make the loudest sound that any animal can make.

# Part - II

# PLANT KINGDOM

Just like the Animal Kingdom, the Plant Kingdom too forms a part of the living creatures on our planet, earth. Scientists have traced the origin of the plant kingdom to algae in freshwater. Today, we have around **300, 000 species of plants** that adorn our planet. Plants give us **oxygen** and they also provide **food** to humans and animals. Similar to the Animal Kingdom, plants also reproduce and are classified based on their similarities, for example, **Terrestrial plants** (plants that grow on land) and **Aquatic plants** (plants that grow in water).

Read ahead to find more interesting details about the colourful Plant Kingdom.

# Chapter - 1

# PARTS OF A PLANT

A plant can be divided into the following two main parts:

(i) Root

(ii) Shoot

## (i) Root

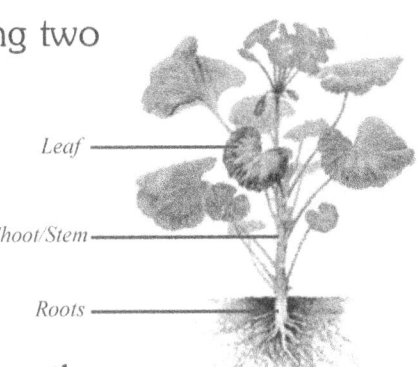

*Plant Parts*

The root is the part of the plant under the ground. It holds the plant firmly to the ground, absorbs water and minerals from the soil, and sends it to different parts of the plant. Some roots like radish and carrots store food in them.

There are two different types of roots:

- Tap root
- Fibrous root

**Tap root:** Tap root has one main root, broad on the part attached to the plant and narrower at the other. It has many small roots growing on its side. Plants like mustard, radish and beans have a tap root system.

*A Tap Root*

**Fibrous root:** Fibrous roots look like a bunch of many thin roots. Rice, wheat and onions have a fibrous root system.

## (ii) Shoot

The shoot includes all the parts of the plant above the ground. This includes stems, branches, leaves, flowers and fruits.

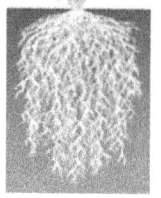
*Fibrous Roots*

**Stem:** Different plants have different kinds of stems, from weak to thick and hard stems. Climbers like money plant have extremely weak stems that need support. They cling on to other plants and buildings for support. Potato, onion and ginger have stems below the soil and they store food in them. Stems support the plant, take the water from the roots and distribute it to the different parts of the plant, thus helping in the process of food production.

**Leaves:** Leaves prepare food for the plant using air, water and sunlight. The tiny veins in the leaf allow the water to get to the parts of the leaves. On the reverse side of the leaf, there are small pores called the **stomata**, through which carbon dioxide gets in and

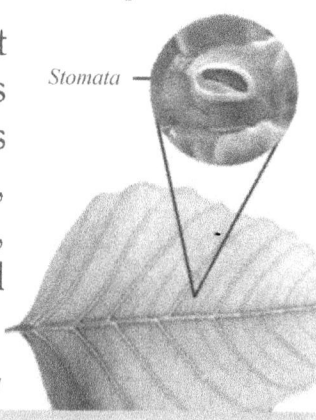
*Stomata*

*A Leaf Showing the Stomata*

the oxygen escapes. Cabbages have leaves that store food.

**Flowers:** In many flowering plants, the flowers form the reproductive organs that contain pollen grains that help the plant to produce fruits. Some plants, such as cucumber, melons and pumpkins have flowers with either only the male parts or the female parts, whereas, others, such as rose and hibiscus have both male and female parts in the same flower.

*A Flower – The Reproductive Organ of a Plant*

A flower can be divided into the following parts:

## Male Parts

**Stamen:** The anther and filament together form the stamen. It produces pollen. The number of stamens and petals are usually the same in a flower.

- ★ **Anther:** This part of the stamen produces and contains the pollen. It is usually on top of a long, hair-like stalk.

- ★ **Filament:** This is the thin stalk on top of which the anther sits.

*Male Parts of a Plant (Stamen)*

## Female Parts

**Pistil:** It includes the stigma, style and ovary.

- ★ **Stigma:** It is the bulblike, sticky structure of the plant on which the pollen grains stick.

- ★ **Style:** It is the long, stalk-like structure on which

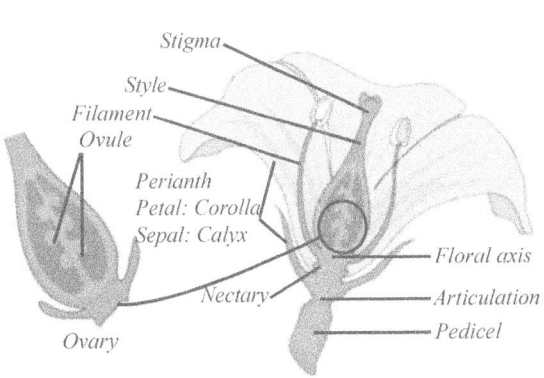

*Female Parts of a Plant*

the stigma rests. It separates the stigma and the ovary to avoid contamination of pollen.

* **Ovary:** This is the seed containing part at the bottom of the flower. These seeds turn into fruits. The ovary contains ovules.

* **Ovule:** It is the part of the ovary that turns into seeds.

## Other Parts

* **Petal:** These are the colourful and bright parts of the flowers that attract bees and butterflies.

* **Sepal:** The green leaf-like structure that covers the outside of a flower bud, protecting it before it opens and blooms into a flower.

*Litchi*

* **Fruits:** Fruits form a covering for the seeds. The seed remains protected inside the fruit and the seed helps in producing new plants.

## Quick Facts

* Saffron used in food items is the dried stigmas of the saffron flower.
* Cinnamon is the bark of the Cinnamomum zeylandicum tree rolled up.
* Rafflesia has the largest known flower in the world.
* Tomato is not a vegetable but the fruit of plant.
* Cabbage and Spinach are leafy vegetables.
* Banana is a seedless fruit.

# Chapter - 2

# PHOTOSYNTHESIS

Every living being requires food. Human beings cook their own food, animals hunt for food or feed on plants, and plants make their own food. The process of food preparation in plants is called **photosynthesis**.

## The Process

*Leaves* of plants serve as a *kitchen*, where the food is prepared. The preparation of food in plants requires the following three things:

(i) Carbon dioxide

(ii) Sunlight

(iii) Water

Different parts of the plant help to get these required ingredients to the leaf. Leaves contain a chemical called **chlorophyll**. This chemical absorbs **sunlight** from the environment and converts it into **chemical energy** that can be used by the plant. On the reverse side of the leaf, there are tiny pores called the **stomata**. This helps to get the carbon dioxide to the leaves. Roots of the plant get deep into the soil and absorb the water and minerals from it. The stem then draws the water from the roots and distributes it to all the parts of the plant. The leaves have small **veins** that help water and other minerals to reach all the parts of a leaf. Using the water and carbon dioxide supplied by the roots, stem and the stomata respectively, and using the sunlight, the leaves prepare the food for the plant. This food is then distributed by the stem and the veins to all the parts of the plant.

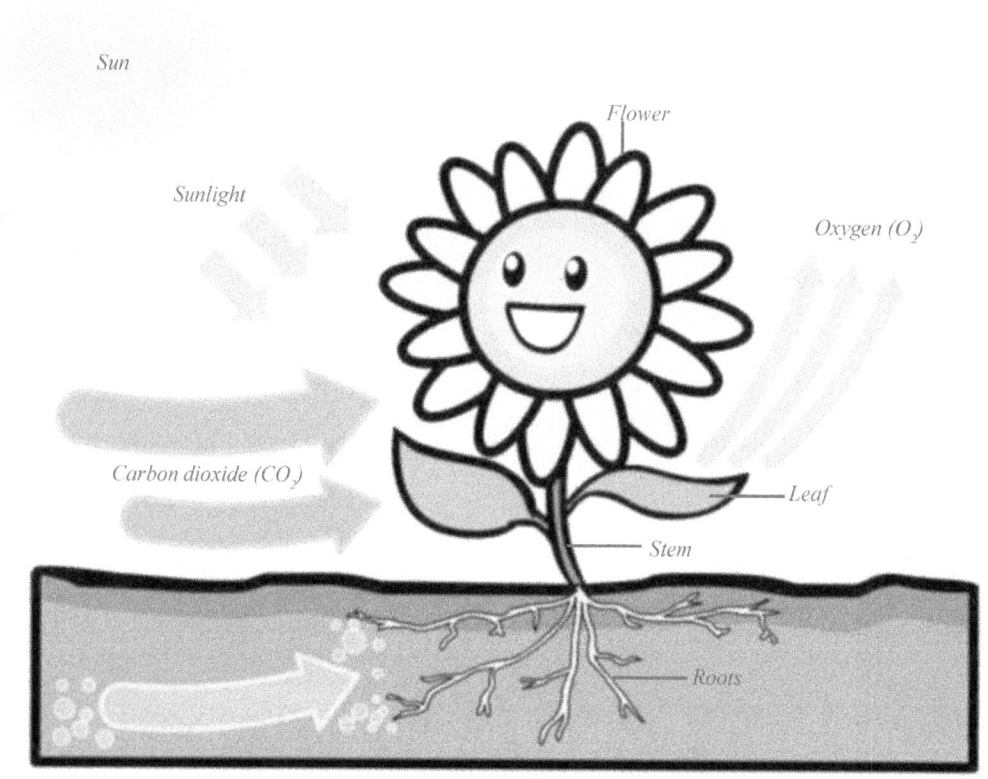

Water and Minerals from the Soil

Food produced helps in the growth and development of *branches, leaves, flowers* and *fruits*. Excess food is converted into *starch* and is stored in the various parts of the plant. All the plants that are able to produce food and contain chlorophyll are called Autotrophs.

## Chlorophyll-lacking plants

Due to the presence of chlorophyll, most plants can produce their own food. However, there are some plants, such as the **fungi** that do not have chlorophyll. They have to depend on other things for their food. For instance, mushrooms, which are a type of fungi, absorb food from the soil in which they grow and bracket mushrooms that grow on trees get their food from the trees. The plants that do not contain the green pigments or chlorophyll are called **Heterotrophs**.

*Bracket Mushrooms*

*Mushrooms*

### Quick Facts

- Every living being requires food.
- The process of food preparation in green plants with the help of water, carbon dioxide and sunlight is called photosynthesis.
- Leaves contain a chemical called chlorophyll that help in photosynthesis.
- Due to the presence of chlorophyll, most plants can produce their own food.

There are some plants, such as the fungi that do not have chlorophyll. They have to depend on other green plants for their food.

# Chapter - 3

# GROWTH AND DEVELOPMENT

## The Seed

Life of a plant begins with a seed. A tiny, lifeless looking seed can give rise to the most enchanting looking plant. Seeds are of the following two types:

(i) Monocotyledons

(ii) Dicotyledons

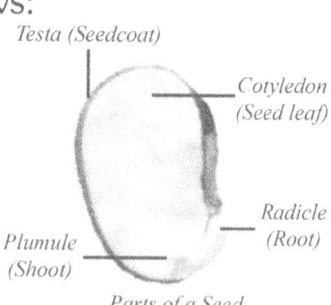

*A Monocot and Dicot Seed*

**Monocotyledons** or **Monocots** are called so as they contain one cotyledon (seed leaf), whereas, **Dicotyledons** or **Dicots** have two seed leaves. The parts of a seed are as follows:

- The seed coat is known as **testa**.
- The young root is called a **radicle**.
- The young shoot is called **plumule** and can be divided into the following two parts:
    - Hypocotyl
    - Epicotyl

*Parts of a Seed*

**Hypocotyl** is the part of the plumule attached to the radicle, whereas, **epicotyl** forms that part of the plumule that is attached to the hypocotyl.

**Cotyledon** or seed leaf is a part of the seed that stores food for the embryo.

Monocots have one cotyledon and dicots have two cotyledons.

The **Endosperm** serves as a food storage in monocots.

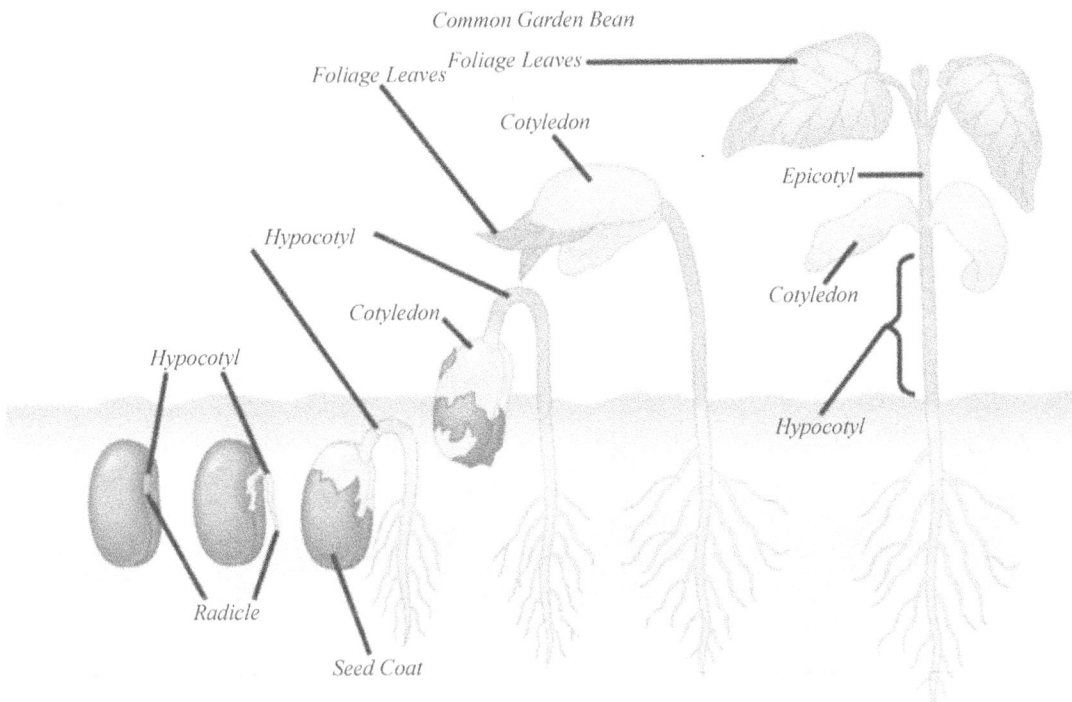

*The Process of Germination*

## Germination

The process of formation of a plant from a seed is called germination. The whole process is divided into stages as explained diagrammatically.

## Germination in Dicots

During the germination process of dicots, when the seed is buried in the soil, the primary root bursts opens the seed coat. The hypocotyl emerges from the seed coat through the soil forming an **arch**. The **epicotyl** is protected by two cotyledons. When the hypocotyl emerges out of the soil completely, it is straightened by the sunlight. The two cotyledons spread apart exposing the epicotyl, containing two primary leaves. In many dicots, cotyledons act as food storing structures. As the plant grows, the cotyledons fall apart.

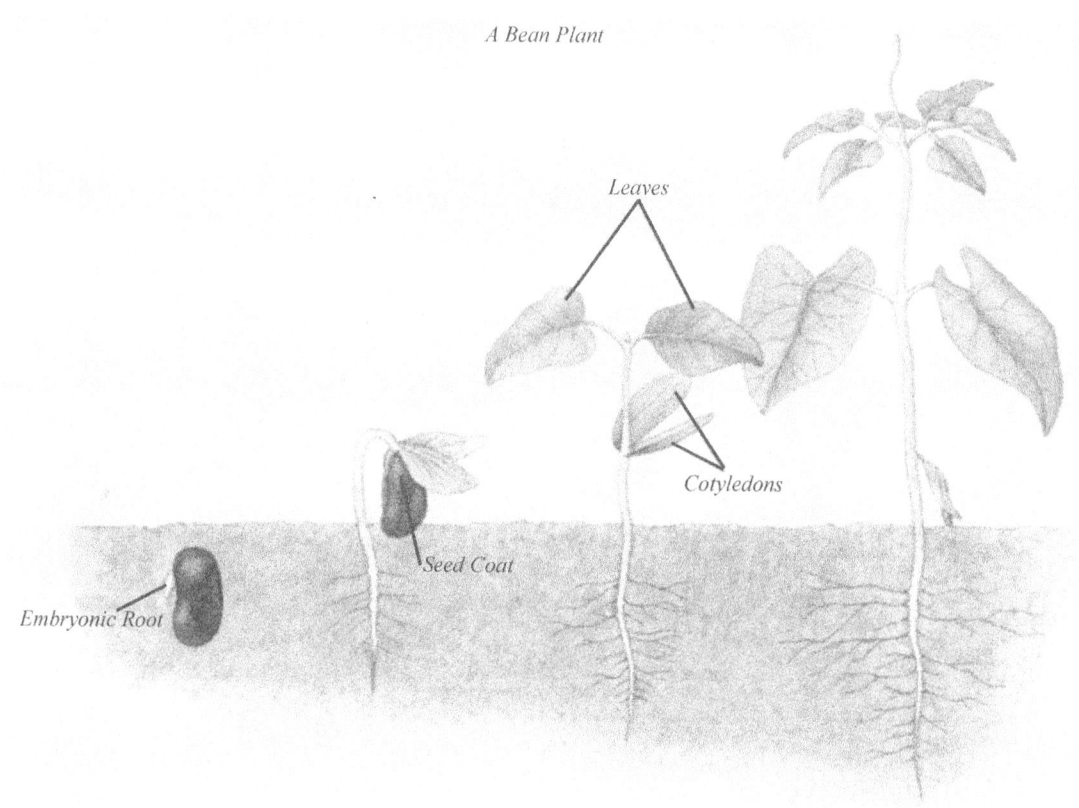

*A Bean Plant*

*Germination in Dicots*

## Germination in Monocots

In monocots, the embryo of the plant rests in the seed and the starch produced during photosynthesis gets stored in the **endosperm**. A seed shows its first signs of germination when it absorbs the water and the radicle (young primary root) bursts open the testa (seed coat). Starch stored in the seed gets converted into sugar, the embryo gets enlarged, and the seed coat bursts open. The primary root develops, giving rise to the secondary roots. The *plumule* (young stem) emerges, producing its *first leaves*.

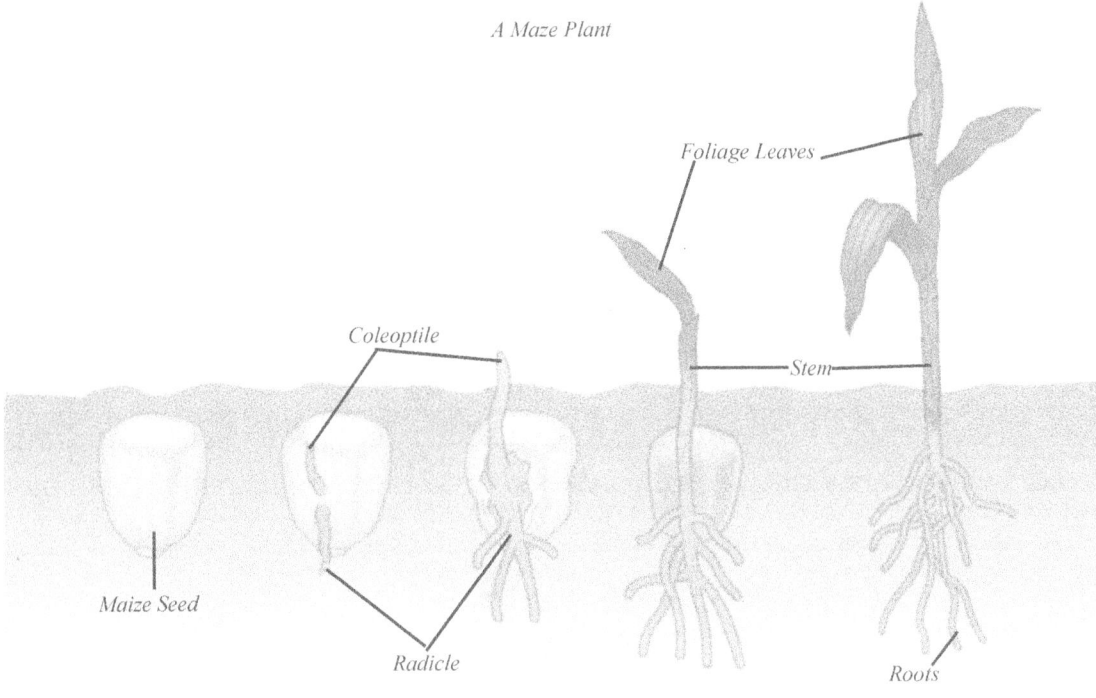

*Germination in Monocots*

## Pollination

A very important process in the growth and development of a plant, besides germination, is pollination. It helps the plants to develop into new ones.

Pollination starts in the flower itself. The stamen of the flower produces a sticky powder called **pollen**. When this pollen is transferred to the stigma of the flower, **pollination** takes place. If the pollen from the **stamen** of a flower is transferred to the **stigma** of the same flower, it is called **self-pollination**, but if it is transferred to the stigma of another flower, it is called **cross-pollination**. Such a transfer can happen in many ways.

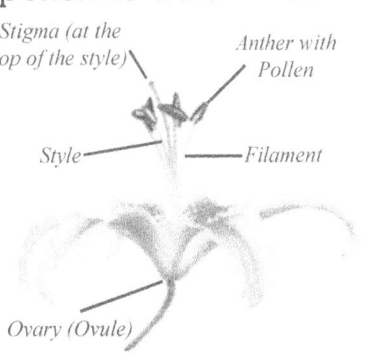

*Pollination in Plants*

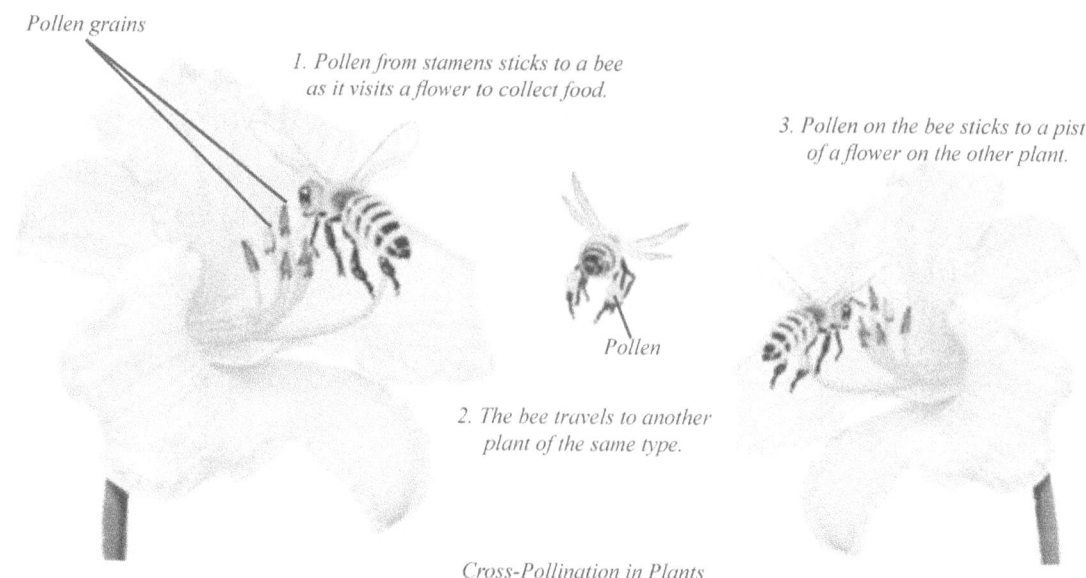

Pollen grains

1. Pollen from stamens sticks to a bee as it visits a flower to collect food.

3. Pollen on the bee sticks to a pistil of a flower on the other plant.

Pollen

2. The bee travels to another plant of the same type.

Cross-Pollination in Plants

Usually, the wind aids in making such transfers. However, animals and insects also play a vital role in making this transfer possible.

Animals Feeding on Plants

56

Bees, moths, butterflies and hummingbirds are attracted by the bright colour of the flowers and when they sit on the flower to suck the nectar, the pollen gets stuck on their feet. When they move on to another flower in search of nectar, the pollen gets transferred from their feet to the stigma of another flower, resulting in pollination. Similarly, when animals come to feed on plants, the pollens get stuck to their bodies and as they move on to different pastures for food, the pollen gets rubbed off their bodies and pollinates other plants.

## Fertilisation

After pollination takes place, the next step is the formation of **seeds**. This process is called fertilisation, which takes place in the **ovary**. The transfer of the pollen from the male part of the flower to the female part of the flower that takes place during the process of pollination leads to the formation of *seeds in the ovary*. With time, the ovary grows into a **fruit**, containing seeds. Once the fruits are **ripe**, they fall on the ground and help in the production of new plants. Thus, the lifecycle of a plant continues.

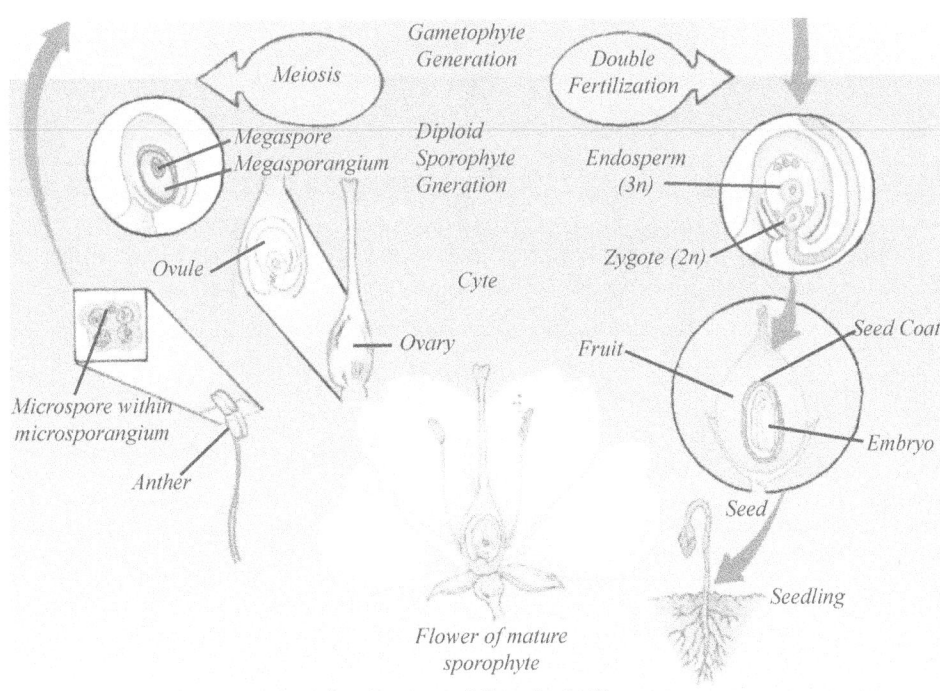

*Fertilisation and Growth of a Plant*

## Quick Facts

- The largest seed is of the double coconut palm.
- Orchids have the tiniest seeds.
- Kiwi fruits contain up to 1000 edible seeds in it.
- Kalanchoe, a type of plant, can grow simply by placing a leaf in the soil.
- The female holly plant do not produce red berries unless there is a male holly nearby to provide the pollen.

## Chapter - 4

# PLANT CLASSIFICATION

Plants are found everywhere, in dry lands, in places with heavy rains, in hot and even in cold climates. They learn to adapt to their environment and the related changes. Plants are known to be classified as **herbs**, **shrubs**, **trees** and **climbers**. However, plants can be placed in the following two major groups:

(i) Terrestrial plants, or plants that grow on land

(ii) Aquatic plants, or plants that grow in water

## (i) Terrestrial Plants

These plants can be further divided based on the habitats, or the natural environment, in which they grow, such as:

- Deserts
- Hills
- Marshes
- Plains
- Forests
- Grasslands
- Coastal regions

## Deserts

*Palm Trees*     *Cactus Plants*

Plants found in the hot and dry climate of deserts adapt to their surroundings by obtaining water from the soil and preventing water loss from the surface of their leaves. It is a known fact that leaves have small pores on their surfaces. These pores are called stomata and the plants lose water through these pores. This process of losing water is called **transpiration**. However, desert plants, such as the cactus, lack such pores. They have pointed **spines** instead of leaves, reducing the loss of water from the surface. Such plants have an extensive root system that penetrates deep into the soil and absorbs water.

## Hills

The hilly regions are generally cold. These areas are usually covered with snow. Surviving in such extreme climate is difficult for any plant. The plants of this region are however capable to

*Pine Tree*

*Cedar Tree*

withstand it. Trees, such as pines, have a conical shape, which helps the snow to slip off its surface. Its pointed leaves protect it from the harsh

Spruce Trees

Deodar Tree

Fir Tree

winters. These plants have **cones** in place of flowers and are hence, often referred to as **conifers**. They are mostly **evergreen** and remain green throughout the year. Some other trees found in such areas are cedar, fir, deodar and spruce.

## Marshes

Marshes are formed of soil in the form of clay. Water gets trapped in the soil particles, making it muddy. The plants growing in these places can survive only if the roots can get fresh air and not get choked with water. Rabbit's foot grass and pickleweed are some of the examples of plants growing in marshes.

Pickleweed

## Plains

Plains have a moderate climate. It's neither too cold nor too hot in the plains. They also receive sufficient rainfall. The plants growing in these regions are **deciduous** or

Maple Tree

**evergreen**. The trees, such as maple, oak, birch, and beech, in the deciduous forests shed their leaves during winter and gain new leaves in spring.

*Birch Tree*  *Oak Tree*

*Beech Tree*

## Forests

Forests are densely populated with different variety of trees, such as the *deciduous*, the *coniferous* and the *evergreen trees*.

*Deciduous Trees*  *Evergreen Trees*  *Coniferous Trees*

## Grasslands

Grasslands are so called as they are covered by grass. The length of the grasses may vary from very small grasses to really tall ones as in the **North American Prairies**, **African Savannas**, and the **South American Pampas** grasslands. The roots of these grasses are the potential source of food for many animals. These are the regions that receive more rainfall than the deserts, making them not too dry, and less rainfall than the rainforests, making them not wet enough for dense vegetation. Hence, the grasslands are generally covered by grass as well as non-woody plants. However, woody plants, trees, shrubs, etc. do grow in some grasslands.

*Tall Grass*

*Woody Plants*

## Coastal Regions

The coastal regions receive high rainfall and the water here is rich in salt content. Plants that mostly grow in these regions are coconut, rubber and pepper.

*Coconut Tree*

*Pepper Plants*

*Rubber Plants*

## (ii) Aquatic Plants

There are three main types of aquatic plants:

- Floating aquatic plants
- Fixed aquatic plants
- Underwater aquatic plants

*Water Hyacinth*

### Floating Aquatic Plants

The plants which float on the surface of the water have to be light in weight in order to float. This is made possible by their spongy bodies full of air.

### Fixed Aquatic Plants

*Duckweed Plants*

Some aquatic plants have their roots fixed to the ground under water. Since the roots are attached to the soil under water, they have to be flexible enough not to get damaged by the water currents. They have hollow stems and broad, flat leaves which help them to prepare their food using air and sunlight.

*Lotus*

### Underwater Plants

Some plants are completely immersed in the water. These plants need to breathe under water. Unlike other plants, these plants have no stomata. They have tiny air sacs in their stems that help them to breathe.

## Other Plants

Most plants prepare their own food. However, there are many plants that depend on other green plants and trees for their food. Such plants are insectivores, carnivores, or parasites. Pitcher plants and Venus flytraps are insectivores, whereas, Bladderworts are carnivorous underwater plants that trap animals for food. On the other hand, Mistletoes are the best examples of parasitic plants. They grow on other trees and suck the minerals and water from their host trees in order to survive.

*Hydrilla*

*Pitcher Plants*

*Mistletoes Growing on their Host Tree*

*Bladderworts*

*Venus Flytraps*

## Quick Facts

- Coriander are Herbs. Herbs are plants that have green and very soft stems as compared to other plants. They are terrestrial.
- Rose and Bougainvillea are Shrubs. They have a thin, woody stem which is harder than that of the Herbs, but not as hard as the tree trunks.
- Plants that have very hard, thick and woody stems, also called as trunks are called trees, such as Mango, Banyan, Apple, Guava, etc.
- Money plant and Bottle Gourd are called climbers as they grow on big trees or on the walls of buildings and houses.
- Watermelon and cucumber are called creepers as they creep or crawl on the ground and do not grow straight like other plants.

# Exercises

I. **Answer the following questions.**

1. What is the difference between living and non-living things?
2. How do the living organisms breathe?
3. How do the living things move?
4. Why do the living organisms need food?
5. How do the plants prepare their food?
6. Why do the living things reproduce?
7. What are two major body systems in animals?
8. What are the main functions of the Digestive and Nervous Systems in animals?
9. Explain the different parts of a plant with the help of a labelled diagram.
10. What is Germination? Explain the process of Germination in Monocots and Dicots with the help of diagrams.

II. **Fill in the blanks with suitable words.**

1. The animal kingdom is broadly classified into _____ and _____.
2. The muscular system helps in the _____ of the body using muscles.
3. Plants can be placed under two major groups: _____ and _____.

4. The process of losing water in plants is called _____.

5. A plant can be divided into two major parts. The _____ and the _____.

6. Seeds are mainly of two types: _____ and _____.

7. A _____ is a place where an animal lives.

8. Depending upon their food habits, animals are divided into three groups: _____, _____ and _____.

9. The process of formation of seeds in plants is called _____.

10. Pine, cedar, fir, deodar and spruce are also referred to as _____.

## III. Match the two columns correctly.

| A | B |
|---|---|
| 1. The seasonal or annual journey of animals in search of better living conditions is called | floating aquatic plants. |
| 2. Water Hyacinth and Duckweed are examples of | Crustaceans, Arachnids and Insects. |
| 3. Lotus and Water Lily are examples of | Migration. |
| 4. Giraffes have no | fixed aquatic plants. |
| 5. Animals that live both on land and water are called | vocal chords. |
| 6. Antarctica is the only continent that does not have | Amphibians. |

7. Tulsi, Mint and Coriander are                    Reptiles and Snakes.
8. Arthropods can be divided into three groups:    called Herbs.
9. The largest flower in the world                  in asexual reproduction.
10. An animal does not require a partner            is Rafflesia.

## IV. Multiple Choice Questions (MCQs)

1. The respiratory system removes _____ which is harmful to the body.
   a. Carbon Dioxide  b. Oxygen  c. Nitrogen  d. Ozone

2. Pollination starts from this part of the plant.
   a. Leaves  b. Flower  c. Root  d. Stem

3. The young shoot of a plant is called a
   a. Plumule  b. Radicle  c. Hypocotyl  d. Epicotyl

4. There are some plants like _____ which do not have chlorophyll.
   a. Rose  b. Hydrilla  c. Rubber  d. Mushrooms

5. The classification of animals is known as
   a. Zoology  b. Biology  c. Taxonomy  d. Ornithology

6. Man is an example of
   a. Birds  b. Reptiles  c. Amphibians  d. Mammals

7. Pitcher plants and Venus flytraps are examples of
   a. Terrestrial plants  b. Underwater plants
   c. Insectivorous plants

8. Chameleons and octopuses have the ability to change colour to merge with their surroundings. This is called as

   a. Hunting   b. Feeding   c. Camouflage   d. Migration

9. Frogs can see what is behind them without turning their

   a. Heads   b. Hands   c. Backs   d. Eyes

10. Fossils over millions of years old have proven that the _____ were one of the first organisms on the earth.

## V. State whether the following statements are True or False.

1. Birds, chickens and turtles lay eggs in which the young ones continue to develop.
2. Fishes breathe with the help of their lungs.
3. Reptiles are egg laying animals.
4. Predators hunt and kill other animals for food, while scavengers feed on the carcass or body of already dead animals.
5. The internal skeleton is called Exoskeleton and the external skeleton is known as Endoskeleton.
6. Insects, such as fly, mosquito, beetle, butterfly, moth, dragonfly, and bee form the largest group of Arthropods.
7. The tall grasslands of Africa are called Prairies.
8. Lotus and Water Lily are examples of fixed aquatic plants.
9. No two zebras have exactly the same stripes.
10. Fishes are the first backboned animals to appear on earth.

# Glossary

**Adaptation:** The act of adjusting to the changes happening in one's surrounding

**Aerial:** Existing or operating in the air as opposed to land or water

**Altitude:** Height above a reference point

**Amphibians:** Animals that live on land as well as in water

**Annelids:** Animals with segmented bodies, or bodies with rings, with no jointed legs

**Anther:** The male part of a flower consisting of pollen grains

**Arthropod:** Invertebrate animals with segmented bodies and no jointed legs

**Aquatic:** Animals or plants that live in water as opposed to land or air

**Arachnids:** Animals with segmented bodies divided into two regions and four pairs of legs but no antennae

**Arboreal:** Animals that live on trees in the open air

**Arteries:** Tubes that carry the pure blood away from the heart in a living organism's body

**Asexual reproduction:** The production of young ones without a partner

**Camouflage:** A form of defence mechanism, where an organism changes its body colour to blend into its surroundings, making it invisible to its attackers

**Capillaries:** The hair-like structures in the body that connect the small arteries and veins and form a network for the exchange of various substances in the body

**Cardiovascular system:** A body system formed by the organs and tissues that help to circulate blood in the body

**Carnivores:** Animals and plants that feed on animals

**Cell:** The smallest component of which an animal or plant body is made of

**Cell membrane:** The outer covering of a cell

**Chlorophyll:** The substance present in plants, giving them the green colour

**Circulatory system:** The body system responsible for the blood getting into all parts of the body

**Climbers:** Plants that have to take the support of trees or buildings to grow on account of their weak stems

**Cold-blooded animals:** Animals whose body temperature changes according to the temperature of their surroundings

**Compound eyes:** Eyes with more than one lens as opposed to that of human beings

**Coniferous trees:** Trees that produce cones instead of flowers

**Cotyledon:** The leaf of the embryo in a seed

**Cross-pollination:** Transfer of pollen grains from the male parts of a flower to the female parts of another flower

**Crustaceans:** A type of arthropods, called so because of their hard outer coverings

**Deciduous trees:** Trees that shed leaves in a season and gain new ones in another

**Defence mechanisms:** Tactics used by living beings to protect themselves from their attackers

**Dicotyledons:** Seeds with two cotyledons

**Digestive system:** The body system that helps in the conversion of food into energy

**Echinoderms:** Marine invertebrates that have outer skin covered with spines

**Echolocation:** A sensory system in some animals that helps them find their ways by listening to the sounds reflecting off from objects

**Ecology:** The scientific study of the relation between animals and between them and their surroundings

**Endocrine system:** A body system that helps to control the activities of the body

**Endoskeleton:** The internal frame of the body of an animal

**Endosperm:** The covering of the embryo in the seed which provides food to the seed

**Energy:** The capacity of the body to perform

**Epicotyl:** The stem that grows between the dicotyldons and the first true leaves

**Evergreen trees:** Trees that do not shed leaves and remain green throughout the year

**Excretory system:** The body system that removes the waste material from the body

**Exoskeleton:** The hard outer covering that helps an animal to protect its soft internal organs

**Extinction:** The condition where a species stops existing or living

**Fertilisation:** The union of male and female organs to produce young ones

**Fibrous root:** A clump of thin hairlike roots

**Filament:** The thin stemlike structure in a flower that holds the anther

**Food chain:** The cycle formed by animals that feed upon the other

**Fruit:** The seed containing product of a plant

**Fungi:** Organisms that absorb food from other plants or the soil in which it grows and lacks chlorophyll

**Germination:** The process in which a seed grows into a plant

**Gills:** The respiratory organs in aquatic animals that help them to breathe in water

**Habitat:** An environment, where an animal lives for most part of the year

**Herbivores:** Animals that feed on plants, trees, grasses,etc

**Hormones:** Substances produced by the internal organs that affect the functions of the body

**Hypocotyl:** Part of the plant embryo in a seed below the cotyledons

**Inhabitant:** The permanent resident of a place

**Insectivores:** Animals or plants that feed on insects

**Invertebrates:** Animals with no backbones

**Larva:** The young one of an insect that does not have wings and goes through a complete transformation as it grows

**Leaf:** The part of a plant that produces food and is usually green in colour

**Mammal:** Animals that feed their young ones using their mammary glands

**Mammary gland:** The milk producing part of a female mammal

**Migration:** The temporary but regular journey taken by an animal in search of food or better living conditions

**Molluscs:** Invertebrates that have soft, unsegmented bodies and often have shells or hard outer coverings

**Monocotyledon:** Any flowering plant with one cotyledon

**Multi-cellular animals:** Animals having many cells

**Muscular system:** The body system that controls the movement of the body

**Nervous system:** The body system that manages the information sent to the body by internal and external factors

**Omnivores:** Animals that feed on both animals and plants

**Ovary:** The female part of a plant

**Ovule:** A product of the ovary that develops into a seed after fertilisation

**Parasites:** Animals or plants that feed on a living, host animal or plant for their own survival

**Petal:** The part of a flower that attracts insects and birds and helps in pollination

**Photosynthesis:** The process of producing food in plants using sunlight, carbon dioxide, and water.

**Pistil:** the organ of a flower that contains the ovule

**Plumule:** The young stem that grows from a seed during germination

**Pollen grain:** The dust like material produced by the anther of a flower

**Pollination:** The transfer of pollen from the male parts of the flower to the female parts through wind, animals, birds, insects, etc.

**Predators:** Animals that attack other animals for food

**Protozoa:** Single-celled organisms that can only be seen under a microscope

**Radicle:** Young root that develops during the germination of the seed

**Rainforest:** A dense evergreen forest that receives a lot of rain

**Reproductive system:** The body system that helps in the production of the young ones

**Respiratory system:** The body system the helps the organism to breathe

**Root:** The underground part of a plant that holds the plant firmly to the soil and absorbs water and nutrients from the soil sending it to the stem

**Scavengers:** Animals that feed on the dead bodies of other animals or plants

**Self-pollination:** The transfer of pollen from the male to the female parts of the same flower

**Sense organs:** Organs that let and help an organism eat, breathe, feel, see, hear, or touch

**Sepal:** The green leaf-like structure below that connects the flower to the stem

**Sexual reproduction:** The process of producing a young one with the help of a partner

**Shoot:** The part of a plant above the ground

**Single-celled animals:** Animals with one cell each

**Skeletal system:** The body system that supports the body giving it a strong internal or external frame

**Spinal chord:** The main backbone of an animal

**Stamen:** The pollen-producing organ of the flower that contains the anther and the filament

**Stem:** The part of a plant or a tree that distributes water gained from the roots to the different parts of the plant and helps in the production of branches, leaves, flowers and fruits

**Stigma:** The reproductive part of a flower to which the pollen sticks

**Stomata:** The small pore-like structures under the leaves that help the plants to breathe

**Streamlined:** Shaped like a boat, broad in the middle and pointed at both ends

**Tap root:** Root system with one main root, broad at one end and tapered at the other, with many thin roots on its sides

**Terrestrial:** Animals or plants that live on land

**Testa:** The outer covering of a seed

**Transpiration:** The process of losing water in plants

**Veins:** The thin tube-like structures that carry the impure blood from the different parts of a body to the heart, or thin hair-like structures in a leaf that distribute water to the different parts of a leaf

**Vertebrates:** Animals with a backbone

**Warm-blooded animals:** Animals that can maintain a steady body temperature and are not affected by the outside temperature

**Wetlands:** Lands with wet and spongy soil

# STUDENT DEVELOPMENT/LEARNING
(छात्र विकास/लर्निंग)

# JOKES
(हास्य)

    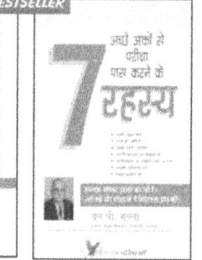 

## MAGIC & FACT (जादू एवं तथ्य)

## MUSIC (संगीत)

## COMPUTER

All books available at www.vspublishers.com

## Quiz Books (प्रश्नोत्तरी की पुस्तकें)

## MYSTERIES (रहस्य)

## DRAWING BOOKS (ड्राइंग बुक्स)

## BIOGRAPHIES (आत्म कथाएँ)

## QUOTES/SAYINGS (उद्धरण/सूक्तिवाणी)

## PUZZLES (पहेलियाँ)

## ACTIVITIES BOOK (एक्टिविटीज बुक)

Contact us at sales@vspublishers.com

# CHILDREN'S ENCYCLOPEDIA
(बच्चों के ज्ञानकोश)

## 71 SERIES (71 श्रृंखला)

All books available at www.vspublishers.com

www.ingramcontent.com/pod-product-compliance
Lightning Source LLC
Chambersburg PA
CBHW080448110426
42743CB00016B/3319